200
HEALTHY KIDS
RECIPES

BEVERLEY GLOCK

SELLERS
PUBLISHING

A Quintet Book

Published by Sellers Publishing, Inc.
161 John Roberts Road, South Portland, Maine 04106
Visit our Web site: www.sellerspublishing.com
E-mail: rsp@rsvp.com

ISBN: 978-1-4162-4574-2
Library of Congress Control Number: 2015947029
QTT.RFCP

This book was conceived, designed and produced by
Quintet Publishing Limited
4th Floor, Sheridan House
114-116 Western Road
Hove, East Sussex
BN3 1DD

Project Editor: Ella Lines
Photographer: Tony Briscoe
Food Stylist: Beverley Glock
Designer: Rod Teasdale
Art Director: Michael Charles
Editorial Director: Emma Bastow
Publisher: Mark Searle

10 9 8 7 6 5 4 3 2 1

Printed in China by Toppan Leefung

CONTENTS

introduction

Food is fuel and children need plenty of good-quality, healthy fuel to help them grow. A nutritious and varied diet can aid the development of bones, muscles and the brain, as well as promote a healthy immune system that protects them from illness and helps them recover quickly.

Children need fat, protein, good carbohydrates and a rainbow of fruit and vegetables to keep them healthy. In order to ensure that children enjoy a wide variety of foods, it is best to introduce new ingredients and dishes to children as soon as you can—even as infants. If they dislike a certain food then leave it a few weeks and try again. There will be some foods that they genuinely dislike but taste buds change as children grow.

When you find dishes that your child enjoys don't wait too long before serving them again. Younger children in particular tend to forget that they loved a dish when you last cooked it and may take a sudden dislike when you serve it again, especially if it contains more unusual ingredients. The trick is to cook favorites on a regular basis. Make more than you need of a recipe and freeze the rest so you don't have to cook from scratch every evening.

Developing taste buds

As children get older—and particularly when they hit the teenage years—their taste buds change again, sometimes quite dramatically. You may find that your 14-year-old who previously refused to eat anything fiery now loves fresh chiles and spicy dishes and suddenly shows an interest in eating salad. Try not to look shocked or make any comment and just go with it—it means you can add more recipes to your weekly repertoire.

The teenage years are also a notorious period of growth spurts and hormonal changes and you may well notice an increase in your child's appetite. Although all children love to snack, it's far easier to control the amount and type of snacks when kids are too small to open the fridge and reach all the cupboards.

As they get older they're more likely to help themselves to whatever they can find, and that often means heading straight for the cookie jar after school. However, if there are some home made savory snacks, muffins, or cereal bars within reach, you can help to make their snacking habits healthier. Recipes that use whole wheat flour instead of regular flour will help fill them up and keep their energy levels stable for longer.

Fallback food

Everyone needs a go-to dinner recipe—something that the kids will eat without question, that adults will also enjoy, and that is second nature to prepare. My ultimate go-to recipe is Spaghetti Bolognaise with heaps of vegetables. I admit that when cooking for small children, I cheat and purée the sauce, so they can't see the extra vegetables that have been included in it.

Sugar substitutes

Sugar is the major source of obesity in children and adults. We don't really need added sugar in our diet, as eating whole fruit will give us any sweetness we desire. Cooking with ingredients such as mashed banana, apple sauce and dried fruit instead of sugar is a far better option than eating processed foods with a high, refined-sugar content.

spaghetti bolognaise sauce

1 tbsp. sunflower oil

1 lb. lean ground beef

sea salt and pepper

1 onion, diced

2 red or orange bell peppers, diced

1 cup/4 oz. chestnut mushrooms, diced

2 medium carrots, diced

1 small zucchini, diced

1 x 14-oz. can chopped tomatoes

1 cup/8 fl. oz. water

1 tbsp. tomato purée

pesto and grated Parmesan to serve

Serves 4–6

Heat the oil in a frying pan, brown the beef and season well as it cooks. Transfer to a lidded casserole.

Add the onion, bell peppers, mushrooms, carrots, and zucchini, to the frying pan. Cook, then transfer into the casserole as they start to soften. Stir in the tomatoes, water, and tomato purée.

Season well, bring to the boil and simmer for at least 30–40 minutes. This is even better if you can cook it slowly in the oven at 350°F for 2–3 hours, as the flavors develop more.

Serve with whole grain spaghetti with some pesto and grated Parmesan on the side.

now try these

chili con carne
Replace the mushrooms with 1 x 14 ounce can of red kidney beans, drained and rinsed. Omit the pesto and Parmesan. Add 1 teaspoon chili powder and 1 square of dark chocolate just before serving. Serve sprinkled with freshly chopped cilantro, with guacamole and brown rice on the side.

cottage pie
Make as before but instead of serving with spaghetti, transfer the bolognaise sauce to an ovenproof dish. Top with mashed potato, scatter over grated cheese and cook for 20 minutes in a moderate oven until piping hot. Serve with green vegetables.

baked potato topping
Serve any leftover bolognaise on a baked potato for a healthy, filling lunch.

Children often crave sugar when they're hungry and the use of "good" fats in the diet—such as extra virgin olive oil, coconut oil, Greek yogurt, nut butters and whole milk—can help to keep them full and prevent sugar cravings. Likewise, replacing sugar with healthier options such as agave, maple syrup or stevia will satiate sweet cravings by providing sweetness without the sugar spike.

Homemade fruit popsicles are packed with vitamins and minerals but have lower sugar content than shop-bought brands—and they are very easy to make. Likewise, homemade popcorn with savory flavors tastes amazing and is much better for kids than the varieties covered in corn syrup. Just try it and you'll taste the difference.

Pick & mix pasta

This super easy supper or lunch dish is another of my favorites. Cook some whole grain pasta and serve with a selection of tasty ingredients that can be added in so your child is in control of creating their own meal, such as:

- Cooked ham or salami

- Cooked chicken or tuna

- Chopped cherry tomatoes

- Finely chopped basil, spinach, and pine nuts

- Steamed broccoli, peas, zucchini, or other green vegetables

- Grated Parmesan or Monterey Jack cheese

- Roast peppers, mushrooms, or onions

- Sundried tomatoes or olives

Children can stir their favorite ingredients into their pasta and can create their own combinations. Encourage them to add a "rainbow" of colors to their pasta.

Pick & mix noodles

Cook udon, egg, or rice noodles, and serve in the same way so children can create their own noodle dish.

Pick & mix egg fried rice

Cook brown rice and mix in a little sesame oil. Break an egg into the rice and stir fry, adding a little soy sauce. Serve with a selection of meats and vegetables as before.

Pick & mix quesadilla

Allow children to choose their fillings for a whole wheat flat bread. Fold it into quarters and fry in a little olive oil to heat through. You could try this with panini, too.

Speedy snacks

- Make fruit interesting without going to extremes by slicing bananas into discs and serving with a little crunchy peanut butter on top. You can do the same with apple wedges.

- Have a bowl of berries, or sliced watermelon or mango, in the fridge ready for kids to snack on.

- Cherry tomatoes and hummus, and crunchy celery with cream cheese or peanut butter are quick and easy snacks that are healthier than anything from the cookie jar.

Fussy eaters

The trick to preventing children becoming fussy eaters is for the whole family to eat the same food. Try to sit down and eat together—as well as helping to encourage children to eat a varied diet, it's a chance to enjoy quality time together as a family.

It can be tricky to eat together every night with very young children, as they tend to need to eat earlier. If this is the case, set aside lunchtimes at the weekend to have lunch together as a family. Always lead by example—if children see parents refusing food they are likely to copy the behavior, as they think it is "grown up."

It is also important to encourage children to help you cook. Children as young as 5 years old can wash fruit and vegetables, and when they're a little older they can peel vegetables and set the table. Older children can become more involved with cooking.

Children should also be encouraged to help you shop for meals. They will be able to select ingredients and learn about new ones. Allow your children to choose a different fruit or vegetable to try every couple of weeks but remember, this means that all the family must try it—adults can often be guilty of avoiding new ingredients, too.

If your child chooses a fruit or vegetable that you don't recognize, find a shop assistant and ask what it is. This is a really good way of demonstrating to your child that even though you may not recognize every ingredient in the world, you are not afraid to ask. If you don't know how to prepare or cook the new ingredient, sit down with your child and look up recipes in books or on the Internet. Make it an adventure to discover together how to prepare and eat it.

Equipment

Most of the recipes in this book require fairly basic equipment such as chopping boards, pans, roasting pan, and sharp knives. However, it's also useful to have the following to help make life easier and the recipes quicker to prepare.

- Muffin pan
- Baking cups
- Loaf pans
- 8-in. square cake pan
- Baking parchment
- Freezerproof and reusable containers
- Grater
- Vegetable peeler
- Potato masher or ricer
- Non-stick griddle pan
- Cookie sheets
- Rolling pin
- Food processor
- Stick blender
- Electric or stand mixer
- Wooden skewers

breakfast

It's important for kids to start the day with a healthy, filling meal and you can choose between hearty egg dishes, wholesome oats, fruity pancakes, and muffins.

quinoa hot cereal

Quinoa is easy to prepare and makes a good alternative
to rice and couscous. Rinse it well in water before cooking
to remove any bitter coating left after processing.

⅓ cup/2 oz. uncooked quinoa

¾ cup/6 fl. oz. almond milk,
plus extra to serve

1 tsp. ground cinnamon

2 tsp. vanilla extract

1 tbsp. flaxseed

2 apples, cored and grated with skins on

2 tbsp. raisins

2 tbsp. agave syrup or honey

1 tbsp. goji berries

1 tbsp. shelled pistachios, roughly chopped

Serves 2–3

Rinse the quinoa thoroughly, put in a saucepan with the milk, cinnamon, and vanilla, and bring to a boil. Cover and simmer for 15–20 minutes, until the liquid has been absorbed and the quinoa is "al dente."

Remove from the heat, stir, and mix in the flaxseed, grated apples, raisins, and half the agave syrup or honey. Stir and serve with the goji berries and pistachios scattered on top, with a drizzle of the remaining agave syrup.

see photo on page 8

NOW TRY THIS

spiced coconut
Add 1 tablespoon shredded coconut,
1 tablespoon grated or crumbled creamed coconut, 4 cardamom pods and ½ teaspoon ground ginger to the quinoa and milk mixture. To serve, stir in 1–2 teaspoons coconut cream with the agave, berries, and pistachios scattered on top.

cranberries & cherries
Reduce the quinoa by 1 tablespoon and cook with 1 tablespoon oatmeal. Replace the raisins with 1 teaspoon dried cranberries plus 1 tablespoon dried cherries. Omit the goji berries and top with chopped fresh cherries or other fresh berries.

berry bircher muesli

This hearty breakfast is full of oats, fruit, yogurt, nuts, and seeds. Prepare the base the night before and leave it to chill in the refrigerator, adding the chopped fruit in the morning. It will keep for 2–3 days in the refrigerator without the fruit, making this perfect for a busy family.

1 ¾ cups/6 ½ oz. rolled oats

1 cup/8 fl. oz. freshly pressed apple juice

1 tbsp. runny honey or agave nectar

4 tbsp. Greek yogurt

4 apples, grated with skin on

¼ cup/1 ½ oz. raisins

2 tbsp. pumpkin seeds

2 ½ cups/1 ¼ lb. strawberries, chopped

1 ¾ cups/14 oz. raspberries

1 tbsp. goji berries

Serves 4–6

Put the oats in a large bowl and drizzle over most of the apple juice. Mix well, adding the rest of the juice if the oats are dry. They should be wet but not sloppy. Stir in the honey or agave, yogurt, grated apple, raisins, and pumpkin seeds. This is your base.

When you're ready to eat the muesli, stir in the strawberries and raspberries, and sprinkle the goji berries over the top.

NOW TRY THIS

summer berry muesli
Replace the raisins with dried cherries and reduce the strawberries to 1 cup/8 ounces. Add 1 cup/8 ounces blueberries, 1 cup/8 ounces redcurrants, and 1 cup/8 ounces blackberries.

nuts & seeds muesli
Reduce the pumpkin seeds to 1 tablespoon, add 1 tablespoon sunflower seeds, and 1 tablespoon each chopped Brazil nuts and hazelnuts.

pear & orange muesli
Add the zest of 2 oranges and replace the apple juice with the juice of 3–4 oranges. Replace the grated apple with grated pear, replace the raisins with dried cranberries, omit the berries and add 3–4 segmented clementines, satsumas, or oranges.

french toast

This recipe is easy to adapt to different types of bread. Try making it with brioche, cinnamon and raisin bread, or a baguette—use whole wheat if possible.

2 eggs

¾ cup/6 fl. oz. milk

pinch of sea salt

butter or coconut oil for cooking

2 peaches, skinned, halved and stones removed

2 tbsp. pine nuts

6 thick slices whole wheat bread

Makes 6 slices

Beat together the eggs and milk. Add a pinch of salt and stir well to combine. Transfer the mixture to a wide, shallow bowl.

Heat a skillet or grill pan over a medium heat and add a knob of butter or coconut oil.

Cut the peaches into wedges, brush with melted butter or coconut oil and lay the peach slices, cut-side down, on the grill pan. Cook for a few minutes until char marks appear and the peaches have softened. Turn over and repeat. Remove and keep warm. Scatter the pine nuts over the grill pan and shake gently to toast. Remove.

Dip each slice of bread into the egg mixture, ensuring both sides are well coated. Add a little more butter or oil to the grill pan, lay a slice of bread in the pan and cook for about 2 minutes until golden brown. Turn over and cook the other side. Repeat with the remaining bread slices. Serve hot, with the peaches on top and pine nuts scattered over.

NOW TRY THIS

stuffed with ham & melted cheese
Carefully slice halfway through the center of each slice of bread to create a pocket. Place a slice of ham and some grated mozzarella or Monterey Jack cheese inside the pocket, press together lightly, dunk into the egg mixture. Cook as above so the bread browns and the cheese melts.

with caramelized apples & maple syrup
Melt 1 tablespoon butter in a skillet. Peel, core and dice two apples. Once the butter is hot and foaming, gently toss the apple in the butter to coat, reduce the heat and cook until the apples are soft and golden brown. Serve over the French toast with a drizzle of maple syrup.

green smoothie

Kids love bright colors and this is a great
way to encourage them to "eat" their greens.

handful of fresh or frozen kale, chopped and
stalks removed

3 kiwi fruit, peeled and diced

¾-in. fresh ginger, grated

1 apple, peeled, cored and sliced

½ cucumber, diced

½ cup/4 fl. oz. coconut water or water

4 ice cubes

Serves 1

Put all the ingredients in a blender and blend well. Pour into a tall glass to serve.

see photo on page 9

NOW TRY THIS

with banana & almond milk
Replace the water with almond milk, omit the ice cubes and add 1 frozen banana, chopped.

with blueberries
Replace the cucumber with a handful of fresh blueberries.

with spinach
Replace the kale with the same quantity of spinach.

with pineapple
Replace the cucumber with ½ fresh pineapple, peeled and diced.

chocolate chia pudding

Raw cacao is the unprocessed version of cocoa so it retains a lot of the nutrients. It also has up to 40 times the antioxidants of blueberries—so great for kids' immune systems.

½ cup/3 oz. chia seeds
1 cup/8 fl. oz. almond milk
4 tbsp. agave syrup or honey
2–3 tbsp. raw cacao powder
1 tsp. vanilla extract
½ cup/4 oz. fresh raspberries
toasted, slivered almonds to serve

Serves 4

Begin the night before and soak the chia seeds in the almond milk. Add the agave syrup (or honey, if using) and mix until dissolved.

Stir in the cacao and mix well with a fork. It will take time but keep stirring and gradually it will all incorporate. Stir in the vanilla extract, cover and chill in the refrigerator overnight.

In the morning the seeds will have swelled and look like tiny balls. Taste and adjust the sweetness, adding a little more agave, honey, or cacao if needed. To serve, layer some of the raspberries and chocolate chia in a glass and serve with a few raspberries on the top, sprinkled with toasted, slivered almonds.

see photo on page 9

NOW TRY THIS

raspberry & pomegranate
Lightly crush 1 ½ cups/12 ounces fresh raspberries, leaving 12 whole, and layer with the crushed raspberries, ½ cup/ 3 ounces pomegranate seeds and chocolate chia. Decorate with 3 raspberries, a few pomegranate seeds and a sprinkling of toasted almonds.

banana, hazelnut & chocolate
Omit the raspberries and almonds, replace with one sliced banana and toasted, chopped hazelnuts. Layer with banana, chocolate chia, and hazelnuts, finishing with slices of banana, and chocolate chips.

breakfast tortilla with scrambled eggs & bacon

Whole wheat tortillas are a healthy choice,
as they are less processed than white tortillas.

3 eggs

4 slices bacon, cooked until crispy

2 tbsp. butter

2 whole wheat tortilla wraps

¼ cup/1 oz. Monterey Jack cheese, grated

Makes 2

Beat the eggs and heat a skillet or grill pan to hot. Break up the bacon slices into small pieces.

In a small pan, heat 1 tablespoon butter. Add the eggs and cook, stirring constantly, until just starting to set but still runny.

Melt the remaining butter in the skillet or grill pan. Place half the bacon and scrambled eggs on a tortilla, covering the lower half. Sprinkle over half the grated cheese. Fold over the top half and fold again into a quarter.

Place the tortilla onto the hot skillet or grill pan and cook for 1–2 minutes until crisp, golden and the cheese has melted. Turn over and cook the other side for 1–2 minutes. Repeat with the second tortilla.

NOW TRY THIS

with ham, mushrooms & cheese
Omit the bacon and eggs. Sauté ½ cup/
2 ounces chopped mushrooms in a little butter.
Place half the mushrooms on half a tortilla,
with ¼ cup/1 ounce cooked, chopped ham,
and the grated cheese. Cook as above.

with mixed berries
Omit the bacon, eggs, and cheese. Spread the
tortillas with 1 tablespoon ricotta cheese. Top
with sliced strawberries and other berries on half
the tortilla. Drizzle with agave or maple syrup
and fold the tortillas into quarters. Cook as above.

with bananas & dark chocolate
Omit the bacon, eggs, and cheese. Mash 2 ripe
bananas and spread on half of each tortilla. Top
with ¼ cup dark chocolate chips and fold into
quarters. Cook as above over a low heat, until
the chocolate melts.

with chicken, avocado & lime juice
Omit the bacon, eggs, and cheese. Mash 1 ripe
avocado with the juice of 1 lime. Spread this
over half of each tortilla, and top with cooked,
shredded chicken and a little finely diced chile,
if you wish. Cook as above.

banana, cranberry & walnut muffins

This recipe is ideal for a quick and healthy breakfast on-the-go for kids.

1 cup/4 oz. all-purpose flour

1 ¼ cups/5 oz. whole wheat flour

1 tbsp. baking powder

½ tsp. salt

2 tbsp. rolled oats

¾ cup/4 ½ oz. brown sugar

1 ¼ cups/5 ¾ oz. chopped walnuts

½ cup/2 oz. dried cranberries

2 large bananas

2 large eggs, lightly beaten

1 cup/8 fl. oz. buttermilk

6 tbsp. sunflower or canola oil

1 tsp. vanilla extract

3 tbsp. apricot jelly

Makes 12

Pre-heat the oven to 400°F and line a 12-cup muffin pan with paper muffin cups. In a large bowl, sift together the flours, baking powder, and salt. Stir in the rolled oats, brown sugar, two-thirds of the walnuts, and cranberries. In another bowl, mash the bananas, then stir in the beaten eggs, buttermilk, oil, and vanilla extract.

Make a well in the center of the dry ingredients and quickly pour in the wet ingredients, stirring gently until just combined. Do not over mix. Spoon into the muffin cups and bake for about 20 minutes until well risen, golden brown, and firm to the touch. Let cool in the pan for 5 minutes.

Gently heat the jelly and brush it on top of the muffins, then sprinkle with the remaining walnuts. Serve warm or allow to cool on a wire rack.

see photo on page 9

NOW TRY THIS

banana, peach & almond muffins
Prepare the basic recipe, replacing the vanilla extract with almond extract, the walnuts with almonds, and the cranberries with ½ cup/ 4 ounces chopped, canned, or fresh peaches.

banana & pecan muffins
Prepare the basic recipe, replacing the cranberries and walnuts with ½ cup/3 ounces semisweet chocolate chips and ¾ cup/3 ounces chopped pecans.

banana, cranberry & walnut muffins
Prepare the basic recipe, replacing the whole wheat flour with all-purpose flour.

herb omelet with tomato

This classic French omelet is simple to make and full of bright flavors.
Don't be tempted to substitute dried herbs in this recipe.

2 eggs

1 egg white

2 tbsp. water

1 tbsp. fresh chives, thinly sliced

½ tbsp. fresh parsley, chopped

½ tbsp. fresh chervil, chopped

1 tsp. fresh tarragon, chopped

1 tsp. low-fat butter, to cook

1 large tomato, skinned, seeded, and chopped

salt and black pepper

Makes 2 servings

Pre-heat the broiler. Break the eggs into a small bowl, add the egg white, and beat with a fork until smooth. Stir in the water and herbs, and season generously.

Melt the butter in a medium ovenproof skillet, tilting to coat the bottom of the pan with melted butter. Pour in the beaten eggs and stir gently at the edge of the pan, drawing the mixture from the sides to the center. When the egg has almost set on the top, remove from the heat.

Put the chopped tomato along the center, then put the pan under a hot broiler for about 3 minutes to just set. Fold a third of the omelet into the center, followed by the opposite side. Cut in half and slide onto warmed plates.

see photo on page 9

NOW TRY THIS

Mexican omelet
Follow the basic recipe, using 1 tablespoon chopped fresh cilantro instead of the chervil and tarragon, and adding 1 chopped jalapeño chile. With the tomato, add 2 tablespoons each chopped red bell pepper and red onion, and 1 tablespoon chopped cilantro and paprika or cayenne to taste. Top the folded omelet with 2 tablespoons sour cream.

herb omelet with mushrooms
Heat 1 teaspoon canola oil in the skillet and cook ½ cup/2 ounces sliced mushrooms for about 2 minutes, until soft. Remove the mushrooms and keep warm. Cook the omelet as directed, topping it with the mushrooms instead of the tomato.

buckwheat pancakes

Whole grain flour adds extra fiber and slow release energy,
which helps to avoid sudden dips in energy levels.

1 cup/5 oz. buckwheat flour
1 tsp. baking powder
pinch of salt
¾ cup/6 fl. oz. milk (dairy, soy, or almond)
2 eggs
butter or coconut oil for cooking
1 cup/8 oz. strawberries, sliced
4 tbsp. Greek yogurt
agave or maple syrup to serve (optional)

Makes 4-6

Place the flour, baking powder, and salt in a bowl and make a well in the center.

Lightly whisk together the milk and eggs. Gradually add the egg mixture to the flour, whisking constantly, until it has combined. The batter should be a thick dropping consistency—add a little more milk if it is too thick. Cover the batter with plastic wrap and allow to rest in the refrigerator for 30–40 minutes before cooking.

Heat a knob of butter or coconut oil in a hot skillet and pour in 1 ½ tablespoons of batter. Move the pan around to create an even pancake. Cook for 2–3 minutes until bubbling then toss or flip the pancake and cook the other side for 1–2 minutes until golden brown.

Transfer to a warm plate and cover with aluminum foil to keep warm. Repeat with the remaining mixture. Serve with sliced strawberries, a spoonful of Greek yogurt, and a drizzle of agave or maple syrup, if wished.

NOW TRY THIS

with sweet corn, crispy bacon & maple syrup
Omit the strawberries and Greek yogurt. Add ¾ cup/6 ounces canned, drained sweet corn to the batter when combined. Serve with crispy bacon on the side and drizzle with maple syrup.

with banana & dark chocolate
Omit the strawberries and Greek yogurt. Slice 2 bananas into rounds. Make a chocolate sauce by melting ¼ cup/2 ounces dark chocolate with 1 tablespoon unsalted butter and 1 tablespoon agave or maple syrup. Mix well and serve drizzled over the pancakes and banana.

whole wheat waffles

You'll need a waffle iron to make these. The whole wheat flour
adds a nutty flavor to the waffles—if you wish, you can use
half whole wheat flour and half all-purpose flour.

1 ½ cups/7 ½ oz. whole wheat flour

2 tsp. baking powder

pinch of salt

1 ½ cups/12 fl. oz. milk
(dairy, soy, or almond)

2 eggs

1 tbsp. agave or maple syrup

¼ cup/2 fl. oz. melted butter,
plus extra for cooking

½ tsp. ground cinnamon

2 cups/8 oz. blueberries

maple syrup to serve

Makes 4

Pre-heat a waffle iron.

Place the flour, baking powder, and salt in a bowl and make a well in the center.

Lightly whisk together the milk, eggs, agave or maple syrup, melted butter, and cinnamon. Gradually add the wet mixture to the flour, whisking constantly, until it has combined with the flour.

Add a little butter to the waffle iron and pour a ladleful of batter into the center of the iron. Follow the manufacturers' cooking instructions.

Transfer the waffle to a warm plate and cover with aluminum foil to keep warm. Repeat with the remaining mixture. Serve with fresh blueberries and a drizzle of maple syrup.

NOW TRY THIS

with cinnamon cottage cheese & fresh berries
Mix 1 cup/8 ounces cottage cheese with 1 teaspoon ground cinnamon. Sprinkle 1 cup/8 ounces fresh mixed berries with ground cinnamon. Serve the waffles with the berries and cottage cheese.

with dark cherries & ricotta cream
Pit and chop 1 cup/8 ounces dark cherries. Mix 1 cup/8 ounces ricotta cheese with 1 tablespoon maple syrup and ¼ teaspoon ground cinnamon. Serve the waffles with the cherries and ricotta.

lunch

From wraps and sandwiches to eat on the go,
to hearty soups and homemade baked beans to
enjoy at your table, these healthy lunch options offer
something for everyone's taste, and schedule.

mini minestrone

This healthy, hearty soup is great for cold weather. Cut toast or bread fingers to serve with it—kids will love to dunk these into the soup and eat them with their hands.

2 onions

2 red bell peppers

1 tbsp. olive oil

1 zucchini

2 carrots, peeled

2 x 8-oz. cans chopped tomatoes, with their juice

3 cups/1 ½ pt. low-sodium vegetable or chicken stock

½ cup/2 oz. very small pasta or spaghetti, broken into small pieces

Makes 4 portions

Wash, peel, and chop the onions and peppers. Heat the oil in a skillet, add the onion and pepper and sauté over a gentle heat for 6–7 minutes, until soft. Transfer to a saucepan.

Wash and grate the zucchini and carrots and add them to the saucepan. Add the canned tomatoes and stock. Bring to a boil. Cover and simmer for 20 minutes.

Return to the pan, add the pasta and cook for a further 10 minutes, until the pasta is soft.

see photo on page 25

NOW TRY THIS

minestrone with cheese croutons
Prepare the basic recipe. Cut a few thin slices of cheddar or another hard cheese. Toast 2 slices white bread under the broiler, turn over, lay the cheese on the untoasted side, and toast until the cheese melts and begins to bubble. Cut into fingers or cubes and float on top of each soup serving.

minestrone with meatballs
Prepare the basic recipe. While the soup is cooking, roll ⅓ pound lean ground beef, lamb, or pork into walnut-sized balls. Fry the meatballs in a nonstick skillet for 5–6 minutes, until cooked through. Add the meatballs to the soup just before serving.

mackerel pâté

Store-bought smoked mackerel fillets make this a quick and easy pâté. Make sure you remove all the bones and skin. Oily fish contains many wonderful nutrients, so it is good for children to develop a taste for it. Serve with sliced pita bread or carrot and cucumber sticks.

2 mackerel fillets, all bones and skin removed
½ cup/4 oz. cream cheese
2 tsp. finely chopped fresh chives
pinch of cayenne pepper
grated zest and juice of ½ lemon
Makes 4 small portions

Flake the mackerel into a bowl, add the rest of the ingredients, and purée.

Cover with kitchen film and refrigerate. The pâté will keep for up to 3 days in the refrigerator.

see photo on page 25

NOW TRY THIS

mackerel & tomato pâté
Prepare the basic recipe, adding 1 teaspoon tomato paste.

sardine pâté
Prepare the basic recipe, replacing the mackerel with 2 small cans of sardines in tomato sauce. Make sure you first remove the bones.

tuna pâté
Prepare the basic recipe, replacing the mackerel with 2 small cans of tuna in water, drained.

salmon pâté
Prepare the basic recipe, replacing the mackerel with 2 cooked salmon fillets or 2 small cans of salmon, drained.

egg foo yung wraps

Egg foo yung are thin omelets that can be eaten on their own or as an alternative to flour tortillas. They are full of protein, naturally gluten-free, and they can be eaten hot or cold.

3 tbsp. sunflower or coconut oil

¼ cup/1 oz. shiitake or mini portabella or crimini mushrooms, chopped

1 red bell pepper, deseeded and diced

5 eggs, lightly beaten

sea salt and freshly ground black pepper

dash of soy or Worcestershire sauce

1 tsp. chipotle paste (optional)

Makes 2 wraps

Heat 1 tablespoon of oil in a skillet, add the chopped mushrooms and pepper, and stir-fry for 3–4 minutes, until starting to soften. Transfer to a plate.

Heat another 1 tablespoon of oil in the skillet, season the beaten egg, add the soy or Worcestershire sauce and stir well. Pour half the egg mixture into the skillet, swirling to coat the base.

Cook for 1 minute until the eggs are golden brown underneath. Flip the egg like a pancake and cook for 1 minute on the other side. Transfer to a warm plate. Repeat with the remaining mixture.

Spread the chipotle paste (if using) over the egg foo yung. Top with the pepper and mushrooms, roll into a sausage shape, cut in half and serve with salad leaves.

NOW TRY THIS

with smoked salmon, cream cheese & dill
Omit the mushrooms, pepper and chipotle paste. Mix together ½ cup/3 ounces chopped smoked salmon, 1 tablespoon cream cheese and 2 teaspoons freshly chopped dill. Spread on the egg foo yung, roll up and scatter over another ½ cup/3 ounces chopped smoked salmon and a squeeze of lemon juice.

with Parma ham & semi-dried tomato
Replace the mushrooms and pepper with ½ cup/3 ounces Parma ham and ½ cup/ 3 ounces diced semi-dried tomatoes. Omit the chipotle paste.

super pasta salad

Use whole wheat or spelt pasta, or replace with gluten-free pasta if required. Keep the pasta chilled until ready to serve and ensure any leftovers are kept chilled in the refrigerator.

3 cups/10½ oz. whole wheat or spelt penne or fusilli pasta

1 cup/6 oz. zucchini, grated

1 cup/6 oz. broccoli florets

1 cup/5 oz. fresh or frozen peas

1 cup/7 oz. cherry tomatoes, chopped

3 tbsp. pesto

5 tbsp. extra virgin olive oil

juice of 2 lemons

handful of fresh basil leaves, chopped

sea salt and freshly ground black pepper

2 tbsp. pine nuts

Parmesan cheese shavings, to serve

Serves 4–6

Cook the pasta in plenty of salted, boiling water, according to the packet instructions, until al dente. Drain and refresh in iced water to reduce the temperature as quickly as possible. Once cold, stir in the grated zucchini, cover with plastic wrap and place in the refrigerator.

Steam the broccoli and peas until tender. Refresh in iced water. When cold, stir into the pasta with the cherry tomatoes.

Lightly whisk together the pesto, olive oil, and lemon juice in a bowl. Add the basil and season well. Pour over the pasta and stir to mix. Keep chilled in the refrigerator until ready to serve then scatter over the pine nuts and Parmesan shavings.

NOW TRY THIS

with spinach & basil pesto
Omit the pesto. Place 2 cups/2 ounces fresh spinach, 2 cups/2 ounces fresh basil, 1 large garlic clove, and 2 tablespoons pine nuts in a food processor. Stir in 3 tablespoons extra virgin olive oil and 2 tablespoons grated Parmesan cheese. Stir 2 tablespoons of the pesto through the pasta and keep the rest in the refrigerator.

with roasted vegetables
Omit the zucchini, broccoli, peas, and cherry tomatoes. Dice 1 cup/6 ounces zucchini, 1 cup/6 ounces eggplant, 1 small red onion, 1 red, and 1 orange pepper. Place in a roasting tray and add 1 cup/7 ounces cherry tomatoes. Sprinkle with olive oil and sea salt and roast at 400°F for 20 minutes, until just starting to brown at the edges. Allow to cool then stir into the pasta as before.

turkey & avocado sandwich

A good sandwich can be a balanced meal. This one has protein in the form of turkey and cream cheese, as well as vitamins and minerals in the raw vegetables, and fiber in the bread.

2 tbsp. cream cheese

2 thick slices whole wheat or rye bread

1 slice roasted turkey

¼ avocado, thinly sliced

4 slices tomato

2 iceberg lettuce leaves, shredded

Makes 1

Spread the cream cheese on one side of each slice of bread. Top one slice with the turkey, avocado, tomato, and lettuce.

Sandwich the halves together. Cut in half to serve.

see photo on page 25

see photo on page 25

NOW TRY THIS

warm salmon & avocado sandwich
Broil a 4-ounce piece of salmon fillet for about 3 minutes on each side until just cooked through. Let cool slightly, then use instead of the turkey. Eat while still warm.

turkey, avocado & coleslaw sandwich
Spread the bread with butter or spread instead of cream cheese. Pile 2 tablespoons coleslaw on top of the turkey.

turkey & carrot apple sandwich
Combine 1 tablespoon each grated carrot and apple. Stir in 1 teaspoon mayonnaise and ½ teaspoon lemon juice. Use instead of the tomato.

turkey salsa sandwich
Add 1 tablespoon chunky salsa when spreading the cream cheese on the bread.

hummus, pepper & carrot wrap

This healthy wrap makes a great midday filler and is packed full of healthy ingredients that will keep kids on the go.

3 tbsp. hummus

1 wrap

few drops of lemon juice

pinch of ground cumin (optional)

1 small carrot, grated

strip of red bell pepper, sliced

small handful of arugula, lettuce, or baby spinach leaves

Makes 1

Spread the hummus over the wrap. Sprinkle with a few drops of lemon juice and a pinch of cumin, if using. Scatter the carrot and pepper over the hummus with the arugula, lettuce, or spinach leaves.

Roll up the wrap tightly, then cut into 2–3 pieces. Eat immediately or wrap in plastic wrap or tin foil to transport. Keep refrigerated until it's time to leave.

see photo on page 24

NOW TRY THIS

hummus, egg & carrot wrap
Hard-boil an egg and allow to cool. Peel and slice the egg, then lay the slices over the hummus. Continue as above.

guacamole wrap
Substitute guacamole for the hummus.

hummus, roasted pepper & olive wrap
Substitute ½ roasted pepper from a jar, well drained, for the red bell pepper. Add 4 sliced black olives. Continue as above.

hummus & chicken tomato wrap
Lay thin slices of leftover chicken or a slice of deli chicken over the hummus. Replace the red bell pepper with 1 medium sliced tomato.

homemade baked beans

Baked beans are popular with children and this homemade recipe is lower in salt and sugar than store-bought beans. You can vary the beans or use a mixture of different types.

1 tbsp. sunflower oil

1 onion

1 x 14-oz. can beans (such as butter or small white beans), drained and rinsed

1 tsp. powdered mustard

1 tsp. molasses

1 x 8-oz. can chopped tomatoes

1 tbsp. tomato paste

1 tsp. dark brown sugar

1 cup/8 fl. oz. low-sodium vegetable stock

Serves 4

Pre-heat the oven to 275°F. Heat the oil in a heavy ovenproof dish with a lid. Peel and finely chop the onion, add to the oil, and cook over a low heat for 10–15 minutes, until translucent and soft.

Add the remaining ingredients, mix well, and bring to a boil. Remove from the heat, cover, and transfer to the oven to cook for 4 hours. Stir occasionally while baking.

Store in the refrigerator for up to 3 days.

NOW TRY THIS

baked beans with sweet potatoes & cheese
Prepare the basic recipe. Place 2 small sweet potatoes into the oven alongside the casserole 90 minutes before the end of the cooking time. Slice the potatoes in half, pour the beans over them, and serve with grated cheddar or Monterey Jack cheese sprinkled over the top.

baked beans & sweet potatoes
Prepare the basic recipe, adding 1 peeled and chopped, large sweet potato 1 hour before the end of the cooking time.

spicy baked beans
Prepare the basic recipe, adding ½ teaspoon chili powder.

mini potato & chorizo frittata

A frittata is a Spanish omelet—it is thicker than a classic omelet and traditionally includes potatoes. This mini version is just the right size for smaller hands and can be served warm or cold.

1 cup/8 oz. new potatoes, diced

6 eggs

½ cup/4 fl. oz. milk

½ cup/2 oz. Parmesan cheese, grated

Small bunch spring onions, chopped

sea salt and freshly ground black pepper

½ cup/3 oz. chorizo, diced

Makes 12 mini frittata

Pre-heat the oven to 350°F. Line a 12-hole muffin pan with paper cups or grease well.

Steam the potatoes for 15–20 minutes until tender. Refresh in cold water and set aside.

Beat the eggs, milk, and half the cheese together in a bowl. Add the spring onions, season and mix well.

Place the potatoes and chorizo into the muffin papers. Pour over the egg mixture, leaving sufficient room for the mixture to rise a little. Sprinkle over the remaining cheese and bake for 18–20 minutes, until the egg has set.

NOW TRY THIS

with zucchini & pesto
Replace the chorizo with 1 cup/6 ounces grated zucchini. Stir in 2 tablespoons pesto with the eggs.

with bell peppers
Add 1 finely diced red bell pepper and 1 finely diced orange bell pepper at the same time as the potatoes.

with carrot, kale & bacon
Omit the chorizo and add ½ cup/3 ounces grated carrot, 1 ½ cups/4 ounces lightly steamed kale, and 4 pieces of cooked, chopped crispy bacon.

whole wheat pizza bread swirls

These are lovely for lunch or a snack and the fillings can be adapted to suit everyone. You can add pesto, sweet corn, salami, ham, different cheeses, olives—anything you fancy really.

4 cups/1 lb. 4oz. strong whole wheat flour

1 tsp. salt

1 tsp. sugar

1 tbsp. olive oil

1 packet dried yeast

1 ¾ cups/14 fl. oz. warm water

1 cup/8 fl. oz. tomato purée or pizza sauce

1 red bell pepper, finely chopped

4–5 small mushrooms, chopped

1 cup/4 oz. grated mozzarella

12 basil leaves

Makes 12 swirls

Place the flour, salt, sugar, oil, and yeast in a large bowl and mix well to combine. Make a well in the center, pour in half the water and combine with your fingers. Gradually add more water until the mixture forms a dough that is soft and slightly sticky.

Dust a clean work surface with flour and tip out the dough. Knead for 5–10 minutes until smooth and elastic. Place the dough in a clean, oiled bowl and cover with plastic wrap or a damp tea towel. Leave in a warm place for about 1 hour, until doubled in size.

Pre-heat the oven to 425°F. Knock the dough back to remove any bubbles and roll out to an oblong shape. Spread with tomato purée or pizza sauce and scatter over the pepper, mushrooms, mozzarella, and basil. Roll up the dough along the longest side.

Cut into 12 equal-sized pieces and lay them cut-side up in a greased, square, high-sided roasting pan, leaving room around them to expand. Cover with plastic wrap or a damp tea towel and prove for 30 minutes. Bake for 10–15 minutes until golden brown.

NOW TRY THIS

pizza & pesto swirls
Replace the purée with pesto and add ½ cup/ 2 ounces toasted pine nuts for extra crunch.

bacon & cheese swirls
Replace the peppers with 6 cooked, crispy, bacon slices.

sweet chocolate swirls
Omit the purée, pepper, mushrooms, cheese, and basil and sprinkle ½ cup/3 ounces dark chocolate chips and 1 tablespoon agave or honey over the dough before rolling. Once cut, sprinkle a little Demerara sugar over the swirls before baking.

dinner

Whether you have a few minutes or a few hours to prepare dinner, you'll find a range of healthy and delicious meals that you can enjoy as a family.

eggplant bake

This is a traditional Italian dish. The eggplant soaks up the flavors of the tomato and basil, the cheese melts and it is delicious with lots of crusty bread to soak up the juices.

3 small eggplants
3 tbsp. olive oil
2 ¼ cups/9 oz. grated or torn mozzarella
1 cup/8 fl. oz. tomato sauce or tomato purée
3 tbsp. chopped fresh basil leaves
6 tbsp. grated Parmesan

Serves 6

Pre-heat the oven to 375°F. Slice the eggplants into ½-inch slices. Heat the oil in a nonstick skillet and fry the eggplant until golden brown on both sides. Drain on paper towels.

Place half the eggplant slices in a layer in the bottom of a small casserole dish. Layer with half the mozzarella, half the tomato sauce, half the basil, and half the Parmesan. Repeat, finishing with the Parmesan.

Bake for 20–30 minutes, until the cheese is golden brown and the dish is bubbling. Serve with green vegetables or a salad and crusty bread.

NOW TRY THIS

with mushrooms
Prepare the basic recipe, adding 4 tablespoons sliced mushrooms in a layer on top of the eggplant.

with chicken
Prepare the basic recipe, adding 1 cooked, sliced chicken breast in a layer on top of the eggplant.

with chicken and mozzarella
Prepare the basic recipe, adding 1 cooked, sliced chicken breast in a layer on top of the eggplant, and replacing the Parmesan with an additional 4 tablespoons mozzarella.

with lentils
Prepare the basic recipe, adding 1 cup/7 ounces cooked puy or green lentils in a layer on top of the eggplant.

Moroccan chicken

This chicken dish is great with couscous and
is a treat for the whole family to share.

2 onions, peeled and chopped
1 garlic clove, peeled and chopped
1 tbsp. chopped fresh cilantro
½ tsp. each ground coriander and cumin
pinch of powdered turmeric
juice of 2 lemons
1 tbsp. olive oil
2 skinless, boneless chicken breasts, diced
1 tbsp. sunflower oil
1 carrot, peeled and chopped
about 1 cup/8 fl. oz. low-sodium chicken stock
3 dried apricots, finely chopped
1 tsp. honey

Serves 3–4

To make the marinade, place half the onion, the garlic, herbs and spices, half the lemon juice, and the olive oil in a food processor. Blend to a purée. Add the chicken to the marinade and mix well. Cover with plastic wrap and marinate in the refrigerator for 4 hours or overnight.

To cook, heat the oil in a nonstick skillet. Add the chicken with the marinade, and cook over a medium heat, stirring, to brown the chicken. Add the carrot and the remaining onion to the skillet, along with enough chicken stock to cover the ingredients. Add the apricots, honey, and remaining lemon juice to the skillet.

Bring to a simmer and cook for 20–30 minutes, uncovered, until the chicken is cooked and the vegetables are soft. Serve.

NOW TRY THIS

Moroccan lamb
Replace the chicken breasts with 10 ounces lean lamb leg steak, chopped.

Moroccan chicken with raisins
Replace the dried apricots with 2 tablespoons chopped raisins.

Moroccan beans
Replace the chicken with 1 x 8-ounce can lima beans, drained and rinsed, and 1 x 8-ounce can borlotti (cranberry) beans, drained and rinsed. Replace the chicken stock with vegetable stock.

chicken satay & whole wheat noodles

This dish is lovely served hot or cold. To serve the noodles cold, cook then refresh in cold water, drizzle with 1 teaspoon sesame oil, mix well and chill in the refrigerator until ready to eat.

1 lb. skinless, boneless chicken breasts
2–3 cups/6–9 oz. whole wheat noodles
2 tsp. sesame oil

for the marinade:
1-in. fresh ginger, peeled and grated
2 garlic cloves, peeled and grated
zest and juice of 2 lemons
2 tbsp. soy sauce
1 tsp. honey

for the satay sauce:
½ cup/4 fl. oz. coconut milk
3 tbsp. crunchy or smooth peanut butter
2 garlic cloves, peeled and grated
juice of 1 lemon
1 tbsp. soy sauce
1 tsp. honey

Serves 4–6

Place all the marinade ingredients into a bowl and mix well to combine. Cut the chicken into strips and add to the marinade. Cover with plastic wrap and place in the refrigerator to marinate for 1–4 hours.

To make the satay sauce, warm the coconut milk in a pan, add the peanut butter and heat gently until well combined. Remove from the heat, add the remaining ingredients and stir to mix well. Cool and keep covered in the refrigerator until required.

Set the broiler to high. Thread the marinated chicken onto skewers and broil for 5–6 minutes, turning frequently, until cooked through.

Cook the noodles according to the packet instructions. Drizzle over the sesame oil, stir to combine and serve with the chicken skewers and satay sauce.

NOW TRY THIS

pork satay
Replace the chicken with the same quantity of pork loin.

beef satay
Replace the chicken with the same quantity of beef steak.

mushroom & tofu satay
Replace the chicken with 3 cups/12 ounces button mushrooms and 1 cup/8 ounces cubed silken tofu. Marinate for 1 hour and thread alternate pieces of mushroom and tofu onto skewers.

Mexican chicken wraps

These wraps are packed full of fresh vegetables and chicken, which makes them a great lunch choice for children.

2 tortillas
¾ cup/3 oz. iceberg lettuce, shredded
1 medium cooked chicken breast, shredded
1 small carrot, shredded
½ small red bell pepper, sliced
1 plum tomato, sliced
¼ cup medium salsa
1 tbsp. fresh cilantro, chopped

Makes 4 mini wraps

Lay out the tortillas and put half the lettuce down the center of each. Top with the chicken, carrot, bell pepper, and tomato. Drizzle the salsa down the middle and top with cilantro.

Fold over both ends, then roll up tightly. Slice in half on the diagonal.

NOW TRY THIS

curried chicken wraps
Replace the salsa with a mixture of ¼ cup/ 2 fluid ounces Greek yogurt, ½ teaspoon curry powder, 1 very finely chopped dried apricot, and ½ cup/4 ounces finely diced apple.

Greek chicken wraps
Replace the salsa with ¼ cup/2 fluid ounces Greek yogurt, ¼ cup/2 ounces finely chopped cucumber and ½ teaspoon lemon juice.

French chicken wraps
Omit the cilantro and use shredded celeriac instead of carrot. Replace the salsa with a mixture of ¼ cup/2 fluid ounces mayonnaise, 1 chopped green onion, ½ teaspoon each capers, Dijon mustard, and lemon juice, and 1 tablespoon chopped fresh tarragon.

vegetable korma

Korma is a mild, creamy, curry dish that is a great way
to introduce children to spices.

1 tbsp. sunflower oil

½-in. fresh ginger, peeled and finely chopped

1 clove garlic, peeled and finely chopped

½ small onion, peeled and finely chopped

½ tsp. each ground cumin and coriander

pinch of powdered turmeric

1 small potato, peeled and chopped

1 carrot, peeled and chopped

1 tsp. tomato paste

½ cup/4 fl. oz. vegetable stock

2 tbsp. frozen peas

6–8 broccoli florets

½ cup/4 fl. oz. light cream

1 tbsp. finely chopped fresh cilantro

1 cup/8 oz. whole grain rice, to serve

Serves 2

Heat the oil in a nonstick skillet. Put the ginger, garlic, and onion into a food processor and blend to a purée, adding 1 tablespoon water if the mixture is very thick. Add the mixture to the skillet and cook on a medium–low heat for 5 minutes.

Add the spices, and cook for 2–3 minutes. Add the potato and carrot, along with the tomato paste and vegetable stock. Reduce to a simmer, cover, and cook for 15–20 minutes, until the vegetables are soft.

Stir in the peas and broccoli florets, and cook for 5 minutes. Stir in the cream and cilantro, and cook for 3–4 minutes. Serve with boiled rice.

see photo on page 41

NOW TRY THIS

with beans
Replace the potato with ½ cup/4 ounces mixed cooked beans, such as kidney or cannellini.

with sweet potato
Replace the potato with 1 small sweet potato.

with chicken
Replace the potato with 1 chopped skinless and boneless chicken breast.

with cauliflower
Replace the potato with ½ cup/4 ounces cauliflower florets. Reduce the vegetable cooking time to 10 minutes.

chicken nuggets & ketchup

This homemade version of the classic kids' meal is so much healthier than the fast-food version. You know exactly which part of the chicken is used and the ketchup is much lower in sugar than store-bought varieties.

1 lb. skinless, boneless chicken breasts
sea salt and freshly ground black pepper
4 tbsp. cornstarch
2 eggs, beaten
4 cups/8 oz. whole wheat breadcrumbs
sunflower oil spray

for the ketchup:
4 tbsp. tomato purée
1 tbsp. dark muscovado sugar
¼ tsp. mustard powder
¼ tsp. ground cinnamon
pinch of salt
pinch of ground cloves
1 tbsp. white wine vinegar
Serves 4

Pre-heat the oven to 350°F. Cut the chicken into large, even-sized pieces. Season the cornstarch. Place the cornstarch, eggs, and breadcrumbs in three separate bowls.

Dip the chicken pieces into the flour, then the egg, and then the breadcrumbs. Spray with a little oil and bake for 15–20 minutes, turning halfway, until golden brown and crispy.

Meanwhile, make the ketchup. Whisk all the ingredients together in a small bowl, adding a little water to loosen the mixture, if needed. Transfer to a clean jar and keep in the refrigerator for up to 3 days.

NOW TRY THIS

Parmesan crunch nuggets
Stir in 2 tablespoons finely grated Parmesan cheese to the breadcrumbs.

herbed crunch nuggets
Stir in 1 tablespoon chopped fresh herbs to the breadcrumbs.

quinoa crunch nuggets
Replace the breadcrumbs with 2 cups/4 ounces cooked quinoa.

zucchini and Parmesan fries

These are a delicious and healthy alternative to potato fries and they taste great with homemade tomato ketchup (page 48).

1 cup/4 oz. grated Parmesan cheese
1 tsp. dried oregano
1 tsp. dried thyme
1 tsp. sweet paprika
sea salt and freshly ground black pepper
2 zucchini, cut into 3- x ½-in. sticks
2 egg whites
sunflower or olive oil spray

Serves 4

Pre-heat the oven to 350°F. Mix together the Parmesan, herbs, and paprika and season well. Dip the zucchini sticks into the egg white, then the seasoned Parmesan, and lay them on a lightly greased baking tray.

Spray with oil and bake for 15–20 minutes until tender.

To crisp them a little more, broil for 2–3 minutes.

NOW TRY THIS

sweet potato fries
Replace the zucchini with 1 small sweet potato cut into the same-sized sticks.

carrot fries
Replace the zucchini with 2 carrots cut into the same-sized sticks.

butternut squash fries
Replace the zucchini with ½ small butternut squash cut into the same-sized sticks.

eggplant fries
Replace the zucchini with 1 eggplant cut into the same-sized sticks.

whole wheat pasta bake

This creamy, wholesome pasta bake will be an instant family favorite.

3 cups/10 ½ oz. whole wheat
or spelt penne pasta

1 tbsp. olive oil

1 red onion, finely diced

1 carrot, grated

1 red bell pepper, finely diced

1 zucchini, grated

1 x 14-oz. can chopped tomatoes

4 tbsp. crème fraîche

½ cup/2 oz. Parmesan cheese, grated

½ cup/2 oz. mozzarella cheese, cubed, plus
1 ball, sliced

1 cup/7 oz. cherry tomatoes, halved

bunch of fresh basil leaves

sea salt and freshly ground black pepper

Serves 4–6

Pre-heat the oven to 400°F. Cook the pasta in plenty of boiling salted water, according to packet instructions, until al dente.

Meanwhile, heat the oil in a skillet and sauté the onion for 4–5 minutes until starting to soften. Add the carrot, bell pepper, and zucchini and cook for a further 5 minutes. Stir in the chopped tomatoes and simmer for 10 minutes until the vegetables are soft.

Blend to a purée, return to the saucepan and add the crème fraîche and grated Parmesan. Stir to mix.

Drain the pasta and add to the tomato sauce. Fold in the mozzarella cubes and cherry tomatoes, add 1 tablespoon chopped fresh basil, season and place in an oiled baking dish. Spread the sliced mozzarella over the pasta. Bake for 20–25 minutes until the cheese is bubbly. Chop the rest of the basil, sprinkle over and serve.

see photo on page 40

see photo on page 40

NOW TRY THIS

with artichokes
Add 1 jar of drained, rinsed artichoke hearts at the same time as the cream.

with chicken & spinach
Add 1 cooked, diced chicken breast at the same time as the mozzarella, and 1 cup/10 ounces cooked spinach at the same time as the cherry tomatoes.

with salmon
Add 2 cans of salmon or 2 cooked salmon steaks, flaked, at the same time as the cherry tomatoes.

with tuna
Add 2 cans of sustainably caught tuna in spring water, or 2 cooked sustainably caught tuna steaks, flaked, to the pasta at the same time as the cherry tomatoes.

easy pizza

Home-cooked pizza doesn't get simpler than this. With its amazing quick base, the dough is made and the pizza cooked in well under half an hour.

for the pizza:
1 cup/5 oz. whole wheat flour
1 cup/4 oz. all-purpose flour
¼ tsp. salt
½ tsp. baking soda
¾ cup/6 fl. oz. Greek yogurt
2–3 tbsp. water

for the topping:
1 x 3 ½-oz. jar roasted bell peppers, drained
2 canned plum tomatoes
1 tbsp. balsamic vinegar
salt and freshly ground black pepper
1 red onion, sliced
2 ½ oz. prosciutto, torn
2 plum tomatoes, sliced
1 ball mozzarella cheese, sliced
2 cups arugula, to garnish

Pre-heat the oven to 425°F. Put both flours, salt, baking soda, and yogurt in a bowl. Either by hand or with the dough hook of an electric mixer, bring the mixture together, using a little water to bind. Knead briefly until the dough is smooth.

Roll out to a 12-inch-diameter circle on a piece of lightly floured parchment paper. Don't worry if your circle is not perfectly formed, this adds to the charm. Bake for 10 minutes.

Purée the bell peppers, tomatoes, and balsamic vinegar in a food processor. Remove the base from the oven and spread with the sauce. Season with salt and pepper. Sprinkle with the onion, prosciutto, tomatoes, and mozzarella. Bake for 10 minutes and serve topped with arugula.

Serves 4

NOW TRY THIS

broccoli & goat cheese pizza
Omit the prosciutto, mozzarella, and arugula. Replace with half a head of broccoli, broken into small florets, 12 whole black olives, and 1 ½ cups/6 ounces crumbled goat cheese.

even-faster pizza
Follow the basic recipe, using 4 pita breads or flatbreads instead of the pizza base. Bake for 5–6 minutes.

tex-mex chicken pizza
Omit the prosciutto and arugula. Replace with 1 cooked shredded chicken breast, 1 sliced green bell pepper, and ½ cup/4 ounces cooked corn. Drizzle with 4 tablespoons medium salsa. Serve garnished with chopped fresh cilantro.

green chicken drumsticks

The "green" comes from the color of the marinade. You could use chicken breasts, thighs, or wings for this recipe, and they're great cooked on the grill, too. The drumsticks can be eaten hot or cold.

1 yellow onion, finely chopped
1 cup/2 oz. packed cilantro leaves and stems
2 cups/4 oz. packed fresh spinach
¼ cup/½ oz. packed fresh basil leaves
zest and juice of 2 limes
3 garlic cloves, peeled and grated
2 tbsp. extra virgin olive oil
10 chicken drumsticks
sea salt and freshly ground black pepper
lime wedges to serve
Makes 10

Place all the ingredients, except the chicken drumsticks, in a food processor or blender and process to a paste.

Place the chicken in a large dish and pour the paste over the chicken. Mix well to thoroughly coat the drumsticks. Cover with plastic wrap and place in the refrigerator to marinate for at least 4 hours or overnight.

Heat the broiler to high and broil the drumsticks until the skin is crispy and the chicken is cooked through. Transfer the marinade to a small pan and cook over a low to medium heat for 4–5 minutes, until hot and bubbling. Serve the drumsticks with the marinade and some lime wedges.

NOW TRY THIS

red chicken drumsticks
Replace the cilantro and spinach with 2 tablespoons sundried tomato pesto and ½ cup/2 ounces grated Parmesan cheese. Replace the lime wedges with lemon wedges.

Chinese chicken drumsticks
Omit the cilantro, spinach, basil, and limes. Add 2 tablespoons dark soy sauce, 2-inch fresh grated ginger, juice of 1 lemon, and 2 tablespoons honey. Mix well.

tandoori chicken drumsticks
Omit the cilantro, spinach, basil, and limes. Add 2 tablespoons tandoori paste, juice of 2 lemons, and 4 tablespoons plain yogurt. Mix well.

beef meatballs

These are so easy to make but are always a big hit with kids.
Serve with a simple tomato sauce and some boiled rice and vegetables.
They also make a great filling for sandwiches and subs.

2 lb. lean ground beef
pinch of freshly ground black pepper
3 tbsp. sunflower oil
Makes 30–40 meatballs

Pre-heat the oven to 350°F. Mix the lean ground beef with a pinch of black pepper. Roll the mixture into 1-inch balls.

Heat the oil in a nonstick skillet over a medium heat. Carefully fry the meatballs, gently rolling them around the pan, to just sear and lightly color them. Do not allow them to brown.

Transfer to a deep baking pan, cover with aluminum foil, and bake for 10–15 minutes until thoroughly cooked. The foil will prevent the meatballs from browning. Remove from the oven and serve warm.

see photo on page 41

NOW TRY THIS

pork & beef meatballs
Replace half the ground beef with lean ground pork.

turkey meatballs
Replace the ground beef with ground turkey.

lamb meatballs
Replace the ground beef with lean ground lamb.

spicy meatballs
Add ½ teaspoon ground cumin, ½ teaspoon ground coriander, and a pinch of cinnamon with the salt and pepper.

beef & carrot meatballs
Add 1 small washed, peeled, and finely grated carrot.

shepherd's pie
with sweet potato mash

This British classic is a wholesome meal that's low in fat and high in nutrients—a perfect dish to introduce children to spices.

2 sweet potatoes
1 tbsp. olive oil
1 onion, finely chopped
1 lb. ground lamb
sea salt and freshly ground black pepper
1 x 14-oz. can chopped tomatoes
1 tbsp. tomato paste
1 cup/8 fl. oz. beef or vegetable broth
½ cup/2 ½ oz. peas, fresh or frozen
2 carrots, grated
1 tsp. dried oregano

Serves 4

Pre-heat the oven to 430°F. Prick the sweet potatoes with a fork and bake for 35–40 minutes until soft.

Heat the oil in a skillet, add the onion and cook over a low heat until softened. Add the lamb, season and cook until browned. Transfer the lamb to a lidded saucepan or casserole dish, stir in the tomatoes, paste, broth, peas, carrots and oregano. Mix well and bring to a boil. Season, cover, and simmer for 30 minutes.

Meanwhile, scoop out the sweet potatoes from their skins, mash, and turn the oven down to 350°F. Once the lamb is cooked, transfer to an ovenproof dish, spread over the sweet potatoes and bake for 20 minutes until the potato is golden brown and the dish is piping hot. Serve with steamed green vegetables.

see photo on page 41

NOW TRY THIS

with sweet potato, potato & leek
Reduce the sweet potatoes by half and replace with 2 baked potatoes, mashed. Sauté 1 diced leek in a little butter and add to the mash before spreading over the ground lamb. Top with ¼ cup/1 ounce grated cheese and finish in the oven.

with butternut squash mash
Replace the sweet potato with the same quantity of roasted or steamed butternut squash, mashed.

cottage pie
Replace the ground lamb with the same quantity of ground beef.

fish fingers with tartar sauce

Serve with green vegetables, salad and either baked potato
or zucchini fries (page 50). The fish fingers freeze well.

1 cup/2 oz. whole wheat day-old
breadcrumbs, or panko breadcrumbs

1 tsp. sweet paprika

sea salt and freshly ground black pepper

2 eggs, beaten

1 tbsp. olive oil

1 lb. sustainable skinless, boneless white
fish, sliced into strips

for the tartar sauce:

1 cup/8 fl. oz. mayonnaise

3 tbsp. capers, drained and chopped

3 tbsp. gherkins, drained and chopped

1 small shallot, finely chopped

juice of ½ lemon

½ tsp. mustard

3 tbsp. chopped fresh flat-leaf parsley

Serves 4–6

Pre-heat the oven to 400°F. Mix the breadcrumbs with the paprika and season well. Spread the breadcrumbs on a large plate. Transfer the beaten egg to a shallow dish.

Brush a nonstick baking tray with olive oil. Dip the fish strips in the beaten egg and then in the breadcrumbs, making sure the fish is covered all over. Transfer to the baking tray and repeat with the remaining fish. Bake for 20 minutes until golden brown.

Meanwhile, prepare the tartar sauce. Mix together all the ingredients in a bowl and season well. Cover with plastic wrap and keep in the refrigerator until ready to serve.

NOW TRY THIS

with classic herb crumb
Replace the paprika with ½ teaspoon dried oregano, ½ teaspoon dried thyme, and the zest of 1 lemon.

seeded salmon fingers
Replace the white fish with salmon, halve the quantity of breadcrumbs, and add ½ cup/ 2 ½ ounces sesame seeds.

with matzo meal
Replace the breadcrumbs with the same quantity of matzo meal.

with polenta crumb
Replace the breadcrumbs with the same quantity of polenta.

snacks &
party food

Growing kids are always on the lookout for snacks
but there's no need to spoil meals with this selection
of healthy goodies, and fruity party treats.

sundried tomato hummus

Sundried tomatoes add extra antioxidants and a burst of flavor to the hummus. Serve with a selection of raw vegetables or warm pita bread cut into slices.

1 cup/6 oz. sundried tomatoes in oil, drained and chopped

1 x 14-oz. can chickpeas, drained and rinsed

1 garlic clove, crushed

juice of 1 lemon

1 tbsp. tahini

sea salt and black pepper to taste

extra virgin olive oil

Serves 4–6

Place all the ingredients in a food processor or high-powered blender and process to a purée. Add a little oil if too thick. Taste and adjust the seasoning if required.

NOW TRY THIS

beet hummus
Replace the sundried tomatoes with 2 small cooked beets.

grilled bell pepper
Replace the sundried tomatoes with grilled bell peppers from a jar, drained.

roast onion & Moroccan-spiced hummus
Finely slice 1 red onion, drizzle with olive oil and roast in a hot oven for 10–15 minutes, until softened and slightly charred. Omit the sundried tomatoes and add the onion, 1 teaspoon ground cumin, 1 teaspoon ground coriander, 2 teaspoons paprika and a pinch of chili powder.

sweet potato chips

Sweet potatoes are packed full of vitamins, minerals, and antioxidants. Homemade chips are also lower in fat. Make these ahead and serve them as healthy snacks, as a dinner accompaniment, or add them to lunch boxes.

1 large sweet potato
1 tbsp. olive oil
sea salt
Serves 4

Pre-heat the oven to 400°F. Peel the sweet potato and use a peeler or mandolin to cut it into very thin slices.

Pat dry on paper towel then put the slices into a bowl and drizzle with olive oil. Lay the slices on a baking tray in a single layer, season with sea salt and bake for 5–7 minutes until crisp.

Transfer to a wire rack and allow to cool completely before serving.

NOW TRY THIS

beet chips
Replace the sweet potato with the same quantity of raw beets. Cook as above.

parsnip chips
Replace the sweet potato with the same quantity of raw parsnips. Cook as above.

potato chips
Replace the sweet potato with the same quantity of potatoes. Once the potatoes have been sliced, wash the slices in cold water to remove the starch before drying them and drizzling with olive oil. Cook as above.

carrot chips
Replace the sweet potato with the same quantity of carrots. Cook as above.

kale chips

Kale chips are packed full of nutrients and are
a great alternative to potato chips.

1 bunch kale

1 tbsp. olive or coconut oil

1 tsp. sea salt

Serves 4

Pre-heat the oven to 350°F. Line a cookie sheet with baking parchment.

Remove the stems from the kale leaves, and tear the leaves into 2-inch pieces. Wash and dry the kale in a salad spinner or pat dry on clean paper towels. Place the kale in a bowl, drizzle over the oil and mix well with your hands. Transfer to the cookie sheet in a single layer and sprinkle over the sea salt.

Bake for 8–15 minutes, checking regularly—the edges should just start to brown and you may need to remove some that have cooked more quickly and return the rest for a little longer. Be careful as they burn easily.

Remove from the oven and leave on the cookie sheet for 5 minutes to allow the chips to crisp up a little more. Serve immediately.

see photo on page 60

NOW TRY THIS

chili
Stir in 1 teaspoon chili powder or dried crushed chiles with the salt and sprinkle over the kale before baking.

sweet kale chips
Omit the salt. Mix together 1 teaspoon super fine sugar and 1 teaspoon cinnamon and sprinkle over instead of the salt.

cumin & coriander
Toast 1 teaspoon cumin seeds and 1 teaspoon coriander seeds in a small pan for 2 minutes until their aroma is released. Crush in a pestle and mortar, mix with the salt, and sprinkle over the kale before baking.

soy sauce
Sprinkle with a little dark soy sauce just before serving, or serve with a bowl of soy sauce as a dip.

crunchy roasted chickpeas

This is such a simple and easy dish to make. Serve it as an alternative to chips, or use as a filling for whole grain pita bread with some falafel and salad.

1 x 14-oz. can chickpeas, drained and rinsed
1 tbsp. olive oil
1 tsp. ground cumin
1 tsp. ground coriander
1 tsp. sweet paprika
1 tsp. hot chili powder
1 tsp. freshly ground black pepper
1 tsp. sea salt
large pinch of sugar

Serves 4

Pre-heat the oven to 400°F. Pat dry the chickpeas on paper towels and spread on a cookie sheet in a single layer. Drizzle with olive oil and sprinkle with the remaining ingredients.

Mix everything with your hands and roast for 15 minutes. Shake the cookie sheet to ensure even cooking, and roast for another 10–15 minutes, until the chickpeas are golden brown and crispy. They should be crispy all the way through—if they are soft in the middle, cook for a little longer.

Let cool then store in an airtight container for 2–3 days to keep crisp. If they become soft, roast for a few minutes before serving to crisp them up again.

see photo on page 61

NOW TRY THIS

wasabi chickpeas
Omit the paprika and chili powder and sprinkle 1–2 teaspoons wasabi powder over the chickpeas. Mix well and roast as above.

curry chickpeas
Replace the olive oil with coconut oil, and the cumin, ground coriander, paprika and chili powder with 2 teaspoons madras curry powder.

soy chickpeas
Replace the olive oil with sesame oil. Omit the cumin, ground coriander, paprika, and chili powder and drizzle with 1 tablespoon dark soy sauce. Sprinkle over 2 teaspoons Chinese five spice powder.

pesto mini muffins

These savory muffins are delicious served warm or cold and freeze for up to 1 month. Atta flour is a semi-hard wheat flour used for Asian flatbreads.

1 cup/4 oz. all-purpose flour
1 cup/5 oz. whole wheat or atta flour
3 tsp. baking powder
½ cup/2 oz. grated Parmesan cheese
2 tbsp. pesto
1 egg
1 cup/8 fl. oz. milk
¼ cup/2 fl. oz. sunflower oil
pinch of salt
½ cup/2 oz. pine nuts
Makes 24 muffins

Pre-heat the oven to 400°F. Mix together the flours, baking powder, and Parmesan cheese.

Beat the pesto, egg, milk, and oil together. Pour this mixture into the dry ingredients, season with a pinch of salt and mix well. Don't worry if there are lumps in the mixture, as they will even out during cooking.

Split the mixture evenly between 24 mini baking cups or a greased 24-hole mini muffin pan. Scatter with the pine nuts and bake for 10–15 minutes until golden and firm to the touch.

To check if the muffins are cooked, insert a metal skewer into the center of a muffin—if the skewer comes out clean the muffins are cooked.

Store in an airtight container for up to 3 days or freeze immediately and use within 1 month.

NOW TRY THIS

sundried tomato & mozzarella mini muffins
Replace the pesto with 2 tablespoons sun-dried tomato pesto and 6 drained and chopped sun-dried tomatoes in oil. Omit the Parmesan and replace with 12 mozzarella balls torn in half. Press into the center of the muffins before scattering with pine nuts.

ham & cheese mini muffins
Omit the pesto and pine nuts. Replace with 1 cup/ 4 ounces Parma ham torn into pieces.

feta cheese, rosemary & red onion mini muffins
Omit the pesto, Parmesan cheese, and pine nuts. Replace with 1 ½ cups/6 ounces crumbled feta cheese, 1 teaspoon dried rosemary, and 1 chopped red onion, sautéed until soft.

healthy pizza nachos

These nachos are made using wheat or corn tortillas and they are baked instead of fried. Serve as a snack, or for a kid's party buffet, but watch out— they're so good you'll need to stop the adults from eating them all!

4 wheat or corn tortillas

olive oil spray

1 x 14-oz. jar pizza sauce

1 x 16-oz. can refried beans

1 green bell pepper, deseeded and diced

1 tomato, diced

2 cups/8 oz. grated mozzarella

Serves 6–8

Pre-heat the oven to 375°F. Cut the tortillas in half, then cut each half into 3 wedges.

Spray a cookie sheet with olive oil then lay the wedges onto the sheet and spray the wedges with oil. Bake for 4–5 minutes until starting to crisp.

Remove from the oven and top each wedge with 1 teaspoon of pizza sauce, a little of the refried beans followed by some bell pepper and tomato. Finish with mozzarella.

Bake for a further 4–5 minutes until the cheese has melted. Serve warm.

NOW TRY THIS

loaded nachos with homemade guacamole
Mash 1 ripe avocado with the juice of 1 lime. Make the nachos as above, adding a little guacamole along with the refried beans. Omit the diced bell pepper and tomato. Cook as before.

fully loaded nachos
Cook 1 small, diced onion in a skillet with a little oil until soft. Add 1 diced garlic clove, 1 teaspoon chili powder, 1 teaspoon cumin and a little salt, and cook for 1 minute. Add ½ pound lean ground beef and cook for about 5–8 minutes until the beef is cooked through. Stir in 1 tablespoon tomato purée and a pinch of sugar. Top the nachos with the spicy beef and serve with lime wedges.

chocolate hazelnut popcorn

Sugar is replaced with maple syrup, agave nectar, or honey in this recipe. You can use microwave popcorn or popping corn made on the stove top.

1 cup/4 oz. popping corn

½ cup/2 ¼ oz. roasted, chopped hazelnuts

½ cup/6 oz. chocolate hazelnut spread

¼ cup/2 oz. maple syrup, agave nectar, or honey

¼ cup/1 oz. cocoa powder

large pinch of ground cinnamon

1–2 tbsp. milk

Serves 8–10

Prepare the popcorn according to the packet instructions and remove any un-popped kernels. Transfer to a large bowl.

Gently heat the hazelnuts, hazelnut spread, and maple syrup over a low heat in a saucepan, stirring constantly, until smooth and melted. Stir in the cocoa powder and ground cinnamon and sufficient milk to create a pouring consistency. Do not bring to a boil.

Pour the syrup over the popcorn, stir really well to coat, and serve.

NOW TRY THIS

toffee & nut popcorn
Prepare the popcorn as above. Omit the hazelnuts, hazelnut spread, cocoa powder, and cinnamon. Melt ¼ cup/2 ounces butter and the maple syrup, agave, or honey in a small saucepan and add ¼ cup/2 ounces light muscovado or light brown sugar. Mix and heat on high for 2 minutes. Pour over the popcorn, sprinkle over ½ cup/3 ounces roasted, chopped peanuts. Mix well and serve.

pumpkin popcorn
Make as toffee and nut popcorn but add 1 teaspoon pumpkin pie spice to the melted mixture before pouring over the popcorn.

peanut butter popcorn
Replace the hazelnuts with roasted, chopped peanuts and the hazelnut spread with smooth or crunchy peanut butter. Omit the cocoa powder and continue as above.

fruit caterpillars

Fruit threaded onto skewers to look like caterpillars—who could resist?
Super healthy and simple to make, the kids will love them.

64 seedless green grapes

8 small strawberries or cherry tomatoes

a little royal icing

16 small chocolate drops or currants

cilantro or parsley stalks

Serves 8

Thread 8 green grapes onto each of 8 wooden skewers. Thread a strawberry or cherry tomato on the end of each skewer.

Place two drops of royal icing on the strawberry or tomato and attach chocolate drops or currants onto the icing for the eyes. Hold them in place for a few seconds to stick.

Use a cocktail stick to prick two holes in the top of the strawberries or cherry tomatoes then cut 1-inch sticks of cilantro or parsley stalks and stick one of these in each hole for the antennae.

Use an edible black marker to draw a smiley mouth on each caterpillar. Alternatively, you could use icing eyes instead of royal icing and chocolate drops.

NOW TRY THIS

olive caterpillars
Use cocktail sticks instead of skewers to make mini versions of the caterpillars. Omit the grapes and strawberries or cherry tomatoes, and use green olives for the bodies and black olives for the heads.

cherry tomato & mozzarella caterpillars
Replace the grapes with cherry tomatoes, and the strawberries with mini mozzarella balls.

Draw on the eyes and mouth with an edible marker.

melon caterpillars
Replace the grapes and strawberries or cherry tomatoes with melon balls. Use a mixture of watermelon and orange flesh for the body and green flesh for the eyes—or any combination you like.

watermelon shark

This would make a great centerpiece for a party table. You will need an oval-shaped watermelon to create a more realistic-looking shark.

1 watermelon

2 red grapes or black olives

3 cocktail sticks

fresh blueberries and strawberries to serve

Serves 8–10

Wash the watermelon and pat dry. Cut a slanted slice from one round end of the watermelon so it stands up at a slight angle.

At the other round end carefully cut out a wedge for the mouth and scoop out most of the flesh. Keep the flesh, as this can go back into the mouth when you're finished.

Use a small paring knife to pare away a ½-inch strip of the outside green rind at either side of the mouth gap, leaving the white showing. Cut triangular sections in this for the teeth.

To make the eyes, insert a cocktail stick in each side of the melon and pop a grape or black olive on the end of the stick.

To make the fin, carve a fin shape from the slanted section you cut off the base. Stick a cocktail stick in the top of the watermelon and secure the fin to it.

Chop up the remaining flesh and put this back in the shark's mouth. Serve with blueberries and strawberries.

NOW TRY THIS

smiley face
Use a round watermelon, and cut a section from the base so it stands. Use a melon baller to cut out two circles for eyes, leaving the red flesh showing. Use a paring knife to carve the mouth, removing the skin and leaving the flesh showing.

fruit wands
Use a star cookie cutter to cut stars out of watermelon flesh. Thread different fruit such as strawberries, grapes, cubes of apple, peach, and nectarine, and other melon onto wooden skewers. Finish with the watermelon stars.

fruit lollipop garden
Make fruit wands as above, using butterfly and flower cutters. Cut out shapes with slices of different colored melon. Thread onto wooden skewers of different lengths and stick into the top of half a torpedo-shaped watermelon.

sweet treats

Most children have a sweet tooth but there's no need to resort to store-bought candy—these homemade goodies include plenty of healthy ingredients.

apple & peanut cookies

These fruit and nut cookies are delicious and really healthy. You can create a fruit sandwich by topping the cookie with another slice of apple if you wish.

1 apple
2 tbsp. crunchy or smooth peanut butter
4 Brazil nuts, roughly chopped
Makes 4 cookies

Slice off the top and bottom of the apple. Core the apple then cut it into 4 slices across the fruit.

Spread ½ tablespoon of peanut butter on each apple slice. Sprinkle with chopped Brazil nuts and serve.

NOW TRY THIS

with granola
Replace the Brazil nuts with 2 tablespoons of granola.

with sliced strawberries & dark chocolate chips
Omit the Brazil nuts. Slice 8 strawberries and place some slices on the peanut butter. Finish with a few dark chocolate chips.

with nut butter
Replace the peanut butter with almond, cashew, hazelnut or the nut butter of your choice.

with toasted, chopped pecans & banana slices
Replace the Brazil nuts with the same quantity of toasted, chopped pecans. Top each cookie with half a sliced banana.

rainbow popsicles

Summer treats that kids and teens will love.

½ cup/4 oz. strawberries

agave, rice syrup, or maple syrup to taste

juice and zest of 2 limes

1 mango

3 kiwi fruit

¾ cup/6 oz. black currants

Makes 10 popsicles

Hull and chop the strawberries and blend to a purée, adding a little syrup and a squeeze of lime juice to taste. Pour into popsicle molds and freeze for 30–60 minutes until firm. Leave sufficient room in the mold to add the other colors.

Peel and dice the mango, removing the pit. Purée and add a little syrup if required. Pour on top of the frozen strawberry layer and freeze until firm.

Peel and chop the kiwi fruit and add the juice and zest of 1 lime. Purée, taste and add a little syrup, if required. Pour on top of the frozen mango layer and freeze until firm.

Purée the black currants and add a little syrup to taste. Sieve to remove the seeds, pour into the mold as the final layer. Freeze until firm.

see photo on page 78

NOW TRY THIS

raspberry & blueberry
Omit the fruit, replace with 2 cups/16 ounces raspberries and 2 cups/16 ounces blueberries, leaving 20 whole. Purée each fruit, adding syrup, if required. Layer red, then blue, red, blue. Add 2 blueberries to the final red layer in the popsicle molds so they can be seen through the red.

pineapple & passion fruit
If your popsicle molds are long you could add ½ pineapple, peeled, chopped and puréed with the seeds of a passion fruit stirred into the purée, as an extra layer between the mango and kiwi.

full rainbow effect popsicles
Add additional layers for a full rainbow effect such as strawberry, mango, pineapple/passion fruit, kiwi, blueberry, and black currant.

chocolate & nut
almond milk ice cream

This sumptuous ice cream is high in protein and antioxidants, making it the healthiest chocolate dessert your children have ever eaten.

3 egg yolks

½ cup/4 oz. superfine sugar

3 ¼ cups/1 ½ pt. plus 1 tbsp. almond milk

2 tbsp. raw cacao powder

1 tsp. vanilla extract

pinch of xanthan gum

¼ cup/1 ½ oz. hazelnuts, lightly toasted and chopped

Serves 4

In a stand mixer whisk the egg yolks and sugar together until the mixture turns pale yellow and leaves a trail when the beater is lifted out of the mix.

Heat the milk in a saucepan, whisk in the cacao powder and cook over a low heat until it just comes to a boil. Remove the saucepan from the heat and plunge into a sink of cold water for 10 minutes to cool the milk.

Stir half the milk mixture into the egg yolk mixture, tip the mixture back into the saucepan and stir to mix. Stir in the vanilla and xanthan gum. Return to a low heat, stirring constantly, for a few minutes until the mixture thickens sufficiently to coat the back of a wooden spoon. Do not allow it to boil or the mixture will curdle.

Chill overnight in the refrigerator and churn in an ice cream maker. Stir in the chopped nuts, transfer to the freezer and freeze until the ice cream is solid.

see photo on page 79

NOW TRY THIS

with vanilla
Omit the cacao powder and hazelnuts and add an additional teaspoon of vanilla extract.

strawberry
Omit the cacao powder. Purée 2 cups/ 16 ounces strawberries in a food processor and press through a sieve to remove the seeds. Stir into the chilled mixture.

mint choc chip
Omit the cacao powder and vanilla extract, replace with 2 teaspoons natural peppermint extract and stir in ½ cup/3 ounces bittersweet chocolate chips before freezing.

sugar-free fruit muffins

These tasty muffins are sweetened with ripe mashed banana and maple syrup or agave nectar instead of sugar. Whole wheat flour helps lower the GI content, too.

1 cup/4 oz. all-purpose flour

1 cup/5 oz. whole wheat or atta flour

3 tsp. baking powder

½ cup/4 oz. dark chocolate chips

3 very ripe bananas

2 tbsp. maple syrup or agave nectar

1 egg

1 cup/8 fl. oz. milk

½ cup/4 fl. oz. melted butter

Makes 12 muffins

Pre-heat the oven to 400°F. Mix the flours, baking powder, and chocolate chips together in a bowl. Peel the bananas and mash with a fork.

Mix together the maple syrup or agave, egg, milk, and melted butter. Add this to the dry mixture, then add the mashed banana and stir well to combine.

Split the mixture evenly between 12 baking cups in a muffin pan and bake for 20–25 minutes until firm to the touch.

NOW TRY THIS

blueberry & oatmeal muffins
Replace half the whole wheat flour with the same quantity of oatmeal. Omit the chocolate chips and add ½ cup/4 ounces fresh or frozen blueberries.

summer fruit muffins
Omit the chocolate chips and bananas. Replace with 1 cup/8 ounces summer fruit, such as peeled and chopped peaches, blueberries, raspberries, or plums. Add an extra tablespoon of maple syrup or agave.

apple & cinnamon muffins
Omit the chocolate chips and bananas. Replace with 1 cup/8 ounces applesauce, 1 cup/8 ounces peeled and diced apples, and 1 teaspoon ground cinnamon. Sprinkle a little ground cinnamon over the top of the muffins before baking.

banana bread

This recipe is ideal for using up ripe bananas. They are naturally high in sugar so you don't need to use as much in the recipe. I also use whole wheat flour, which is a slow-release carbohydrate.

3–4 very ripe bananas

1 ½ cups/8 oz. whole wheat flour

2 tsp. baking powder

1 tsp. pumpkin spice

1 tsp. ground cinnamon

½ cup/4 oz. soft butter

½ cup/2 oz. light muscovado or light brown sugar

2 eggs

4 tbsp. maple syrup or agave nectar

¾ cup/3 ½ oz. walnuts, chopped

demerara or raw sugar to sprinkle

Makes 1 loaf

Pre-heat the oven to 350°F. Grease and line a 1.5-quart loaf pan.

Peel the bananas and mash with a fork. Mix together the flour, baking powder, pumpkin spice, and ground cinnamon. Mix in the bananas.

Cream the butter and sugar together until light and fluffy. Add the eggs, maple syrup, or agave, and the flour mixture, and mix well. Stir in the walnuts.

Transfer to the loaf pan, sprinkle over the sugar and bake for 1 ¼ hours. Use a skewer to check if the bread is cooked—if it comes out clean, it is cooked; if not, cook for 5 minutes more.

Leave to cool in the pan for 10 minutes, then transfer to a wire rack until completely cool.

NOW TRY THIS

wheat-free banana bread
Replace the whole wheat flour with the same quantity of gluten-free brown rice flour.

high-protein banana bread
Replace the whole wheat flour with the same quantity of ground almonds, plus 2 tablespoons of ground flaxseed.

pumpkin banana bread
Use 2 bananas and add 1 cup/8 ounces canned pumpkin purée.

banana bread with dates
Omit the sugar and add ½ cup/4 ounces pitted, chopped dates to the mixture.

blackberry & apple flapjack

This flapjack is sticky and moist. With the addition of fresh fruit it is wise to store it in the refrigerator to prevent it from spoiling.

½ cup/4 oz. butter

⅓ cup/2 ½ oz. demerara or raw sugar

2 tbsp. maple syrup, agave syrup, or rice syrup

1 cup/3 oz. rolled oats

1 cup/3 oz. jumbo rolled oats

½ cup/2 ½ oz. sunflower seeds

¼ cup/1 oz. pumpkin seeds

½ cup/1 ½ oz. Brazil nuts, chopped

1 large Granny Smith apple, peeled and grated

2 cups/8 oz. blackberries, washed

Makes 12

Pre-heat the oven to 350°F. Melt the butter, sugar, and syrup over a low heat. Remove from the heat and add the oats, seeds, and nuts. Stir to mix. Gently stir in the grated apple.

Grease and line a 9-inch square cake pan with baking parchment. Press half the flapjack mixture into the base of the pan. Mash the blackberries with a fork and spread these on top of the flapjack mixture. Top with the rest of the flapjack mixture, leaving the blackberries sandwiched in the middle.

Bake in the center of the oven for 20–25 minutes until nicely browned. Cut into squares and leave in the pan to cool completely.

see photo on page 79

NOW TRY THIS

with raisins
Omit the apple and blackberries and replace with 1 cup/5 ounces raisins.

with cranberry & orange
Omit the apple and blackberries and replace with 1 cup/5 ounces dried cranberries or fresh cranberries chopped in a food processor. Stir in the grated zest of 2 oranges.

super nutty & seedy flapjack
Omit the apple and blackberries, replace with 2 tablespoons chia seeds, ⅓ cup/1 ½ ounces chopped roasted hazelnuts, 1 tablespoon lucuma powder, 2 teaspoons acai powder, ⅔ cup/2 ounces shredded coconut or coconut flakes, 1 tablespoon flaxseed, and continue as above.

sweet potato & orange cupcakes

Orange-fleshed sweet potatoes are rich in beta carotene (a source of vitamin A).

2 medium sweet potatoes
½ cup/4 oz. soft butter
1 cup/7 oz. light muscovado sugar
3 large eggs
1 ¾ cups/9 oz. whole meal or self-rising flour
½ tsp. baking powder
¼ tsp. salt
1 tsp. ground cinnamon
1 tsp. ground ginger
½ tsp. pumpkin spice
pinch ground nutmeg
½ tsp. vanilla
finely grated zest of 1 orange
1 ¾ cups/14 oz. confectioners' sugar
juice and finely grated zest of 1–2 oranges
Makes 12

To cook the sweet potatoes, bake in a hot oven (400°F) in their skins for 40–45 minutes, until soft. Split and scoop out the flesh. Do not boil the potatoes as they soak up water and your mix may not rise properly. Reduce the oven to 350°F.

Cream the butter and sugar together until light and fluffy. Add the mashed sweet potato and beat to combine. Beat the eggs and add to the mixture. Sieve in the flour, baking powder, salt, and spices. Fold into the mixture, add the vanilla and orange zest and gently mix together.

Divide between 12 baking cups in a muffin pan. Bake for 20–25 minutes until golden brown and firm to the touch. Cool on a cooling rack.

Sieve the confectioners' sugar into a bowl, add sufficient orange juice to mix to a stiff paste then ice the cakes. Decorate with orange zest.

see photo on page 79

NOW TRY THIS

with walnuts
Add ½ cup/1 ½ ounces chopped walnuts to the mixture with the vanilla. Walnuts are rich in omega 3 fatty acids, and vitamin E.

with apricots & coconut
Add ¼ cup/1 ½ ounces chopped dried apricots and ⅔ cup/2 ounces shredded coconut to the mixture with the spices.

with cinnamon frosting & pecans
Add ½ cup/1 ½ ounces chopped pecans. Omit the frosting and replace with 1 ¾ cups/14 ounces confectioners' sugar, and 2 teaspoons ground cinnamon. Mix with sufficient water or orange juice to form a thin frosting. Drizzle over the cakes once cooled. Top with a pecan half.

sugar-free & wheat-free chocolate chip cookies

These delicious cookies use ground almonds in place of flour and stevia in place of sugar. This makes them super healthy, high in protein and great for anyone with gluten allergy. To make them dairy-free, use melted coconut oil in place of butter and use dairy-free chocolate.

2 cups/8 oz. ground almonds
1 tsp. gluten-free baking powder
1 egg
¼ cup/2 oz. butter, melted
1 tsp. vanilla extract
½ cup/4 oz. dark chocolate chips
¼ cup/2 oz. powdered stevia

Makes 24

Pre-heat the oven to 375°F. Mix all the ingredients together to form a sticky dough. Dip your fingers in a little cold water to stop the mixture sticking to them, then form the dough into 24 balls.

Transfer the balls to a greased and lined baking tray and cook for 8–12 minutes until golden brown but still soft in the middle.

Transfer to a wire rack to cool fully. The cookies can be stored in an airtight container for up to 5 days.

NOW TRY THIS

white chocolate & dried raspberry cookies
Replace the dark chocolate chips with half the quantity of white chocolate chips and add ¼ cup/2 ounces dried raspberries.

oatmeal & raisin cookies (not gluten-free)
Replace the ground almonds with the same quantity of oatmeal and replace the chocolate chips with the same quantity of raisins.

pecan & maple syrup
Reduce the chocolate chips by half and add ¼ cup/1 ounce chopped pecans. Reduce the stevia by half and add 1 tablespoon maple syrup and an extra 2 tablespoons ground almonds.

double chocolate
Add 1 tablespoon raw cacao to the mixture.

peach & blueberry samosas

These are very quick to make and taste delicious eaten warm.
You can make them ahead and crisp them up in a hot oven for
3–4 minutes just before serving.

3 ripe peaches, skins and stones removed,
chopped
1 cup/8 oz. blueberries
1 x 8-oz. pack filo pastry
¼ cup/2 oz. butter, melted
confectioner's sugar, to dust
Makes 10–12 samosas

Pre-heat the oven to 400°F. Mix together the chopped peaches and blueberries and set aside.

Cut the sheets of filo into strips of approximately 4 x 12 inches. Cover with a damp kitchen towel to prevent the pastry drying out.

Work with 1 sheet at a time and brush 1 side with butter. Place 1 heaped tablespoon of the fruit at the top of the pastry strip and fold over one corner to form a triangle. Keep folding down the strip, in the shape of a triangle, until you reach the bottom of the pastry. Dampen the bottom edge with water to stick it down. Repeat with the rest of the mixture.

Transfer to a greased baking tray, brush with melted butter and bake for 15–20 minutes until golden brown. Remove from the oven, allow to cool a little, then dust with powdered sugar and serve.

NOW TRY THIS

mango samosas
Replace the peaches and berries with 1 ½ cups/ 12 ounces fresh mango, peeled and diced.

pineapple & coconut samosas
Replace the peaches and berries with 1 ½ cups/ 12 ounces fresh pineapple, peeled and diced. Toast 1 ounce flaked, unsweetened coconut in a dry frying pan until golden; mix with the pineapple.

strawberry samosas
Replace the peaches and berries with 1 ½ cups/ 12 ounces fresh strawberries, chopped.

caramelized apple & cinnamon
Omit the peaches and berries. Peel, core and dice 3 apples. In a pan melt 1 tablespoon butter and 1 tablespoon light brown sugar. Add the diced apples and cook for 5–8 minutes, until the apples are soft but still hold their shape.